Introduction

World War II was the largest and most violent armed conflict in the history of mankind. However, the half century that now separates us from that conflict has exacted its toll on our collective knowledge. While World War II continues to absorb the interest of military scholars and historians, as well as its veterans, a generation of Americans has grown to maturity largely unaware of the political, social, and military implications of a war that, more than any other, united us as a people with a common purpose.

Highly relevant today, World War II has much to teach us, not only about the profession of arms, but also about military preparedness, global strategy, and combined operations in the coalition war against fascism. During the next several years, the U.S. Army will participate in the nation's 50th anniversary commemoration of World War II. The commemoration will include the publication of various materials to help educate Americans about that war. The works produced will provide great opportunities to learn about and renew pride in an Army that fought so magnificently in what has been called "the mighty endeavor."

World War II was waged on land, on sea, and in the air over several diverse theaters of operation for approximately six years. The following essay is one of a series of campaign studies highlighting those struggles that, with their accompanying suggestions for further reading, are designed to introduce you to one of the Army's significant military feats from that war.

This brochure was prepared in the U.S. Army Center of Military History by Leo Hirrel. I hope this absorbing account of that period will enhance your appreciation of American achievements during World War II.

GORDON R. SULLIVAN
General, United States Army
Chief of Staff

Bismarck Archipelago

15 December 1943–27 November 1944

By the close of 1943, the United States, Australia, and New Zealand had stopped the Japanese juggernaut in the Pacific. To put the Japanese on the defensive, within the framework of the global strategy adopted by American and British leaders, the Allies initiated offensive operations along two mutually supporting lines of advance. Admiral Chester Nimitz, who commanded operations in the Central Pacific, invaded the Gilbert Islands in the Allied drive toward Japan, while General Douglas MacArthur, commander of Allied forces in the Southwest Pacific Area, initiated a series of amphibious assault operations along the New Guinea coast. These operations were the first steps in his drive to return to the Philippines, a pledge he had made when he left the islands in 1942.

Before MacArthur could begin operations against the Philippines, he needed to capture the Bismarck Archipelago, a group of islands off the New Guinea coast. Continued enemy control of the region would otherwise jeopardize his campaign. The struggle for these islands—New Britain, New Ireland, the Admiralties, and several smaller islands—was official y designated as the Bismarck Archipelago Campaign.

Strategic Setting

One of the most important Allied goals in the Pacific was the reduction of the formidable Japanese bastion at Rabaul on the northeastern end of New Britain. With its ample harbor, multiple airfields and natural defenses, Rabaul provided a sanctuary from which the Japanese could resupply their forces in the Solomons, launch an assault on Australia, or threaten the vital supply lines linking Australia and the United States. Its reduction, code-named CARTWHEEL, had been approved by the U.S. and British Combined Chiefs of Staff as a primary objective in 1942 and was reconfi med as a priority objective at the Casablanca Conference in 1943. But despite Rabaul's importance, the Allies hesitated to attack the fortress directly. Its land defenses made such an operation too costly. Within the broad confine of Operation CARTWHEEL, the Allies thus decided to isolate and gradually to weaken Rabaul through attrition and starvation. The Bismarck Archipelago Campaign would then deliver the final blow to the Japanese stronghold.

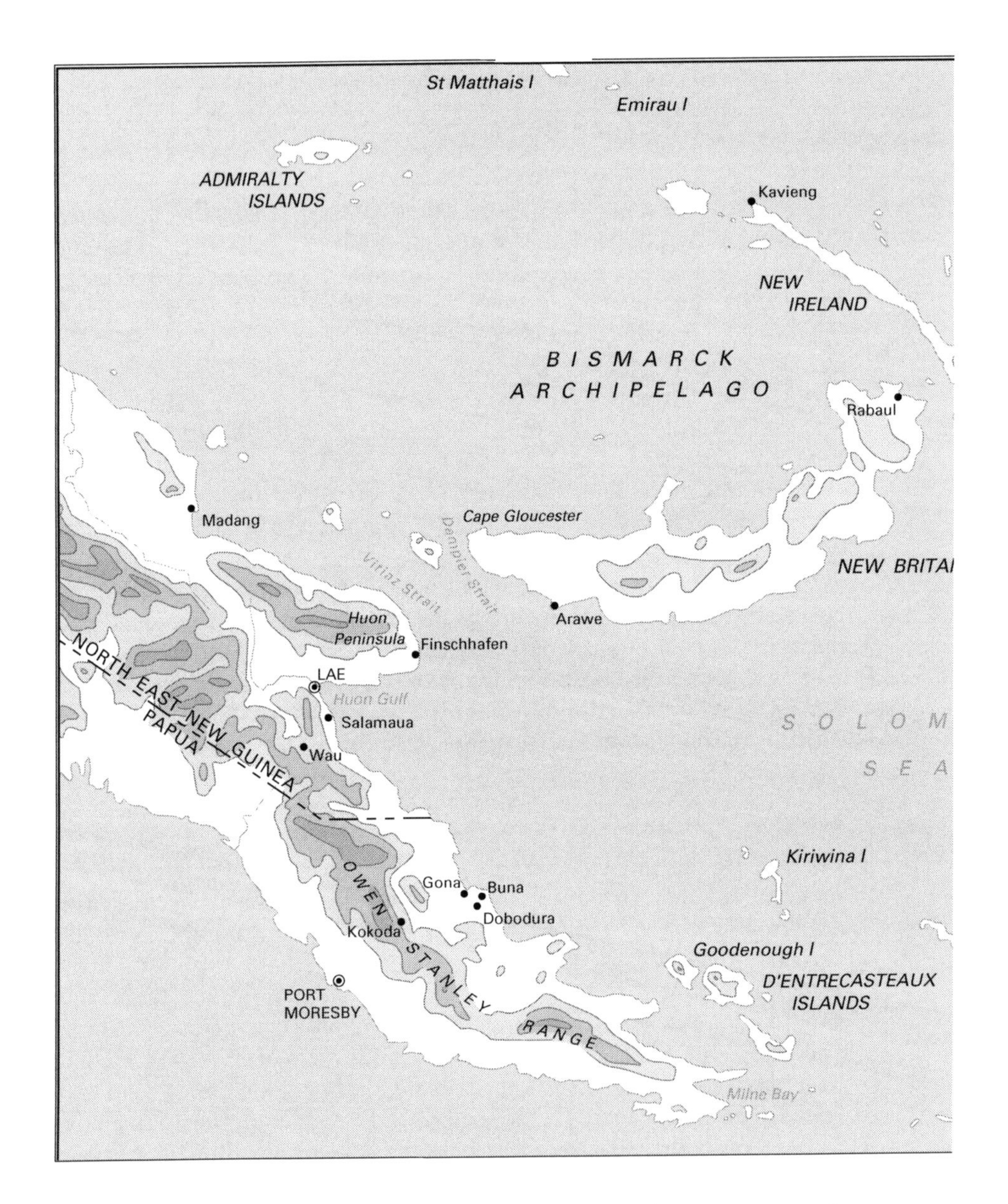

Although the reduction of Rabaul was an important goal, MacArthur was also interested in obtaining bases to support his drive toward the Philippines. All the military services, and especially the Allied navies, required logistical bases to resupply their forces, repair their equipment, treat their wounded, and support their fighting ele-

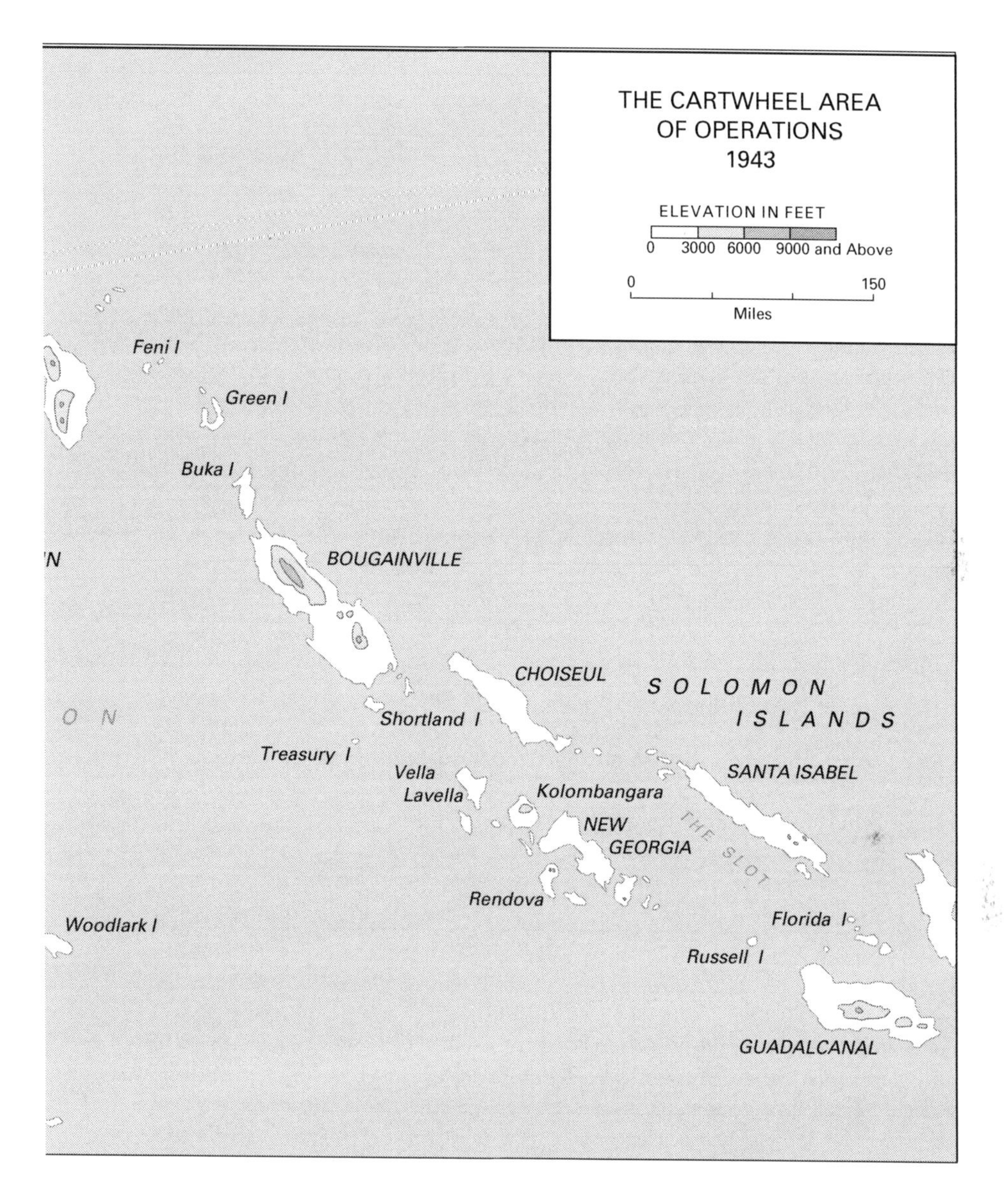

ments. The Admiralty Islands, within the Bismarck Archipelago, contained an excellent harbor that could fulfill those needs

Like much of the southern Pacific, the Bismarck Archipelago consisted of volcanic islands with steep mountains, dense jungles, and malaria-breeding swamps. Temperatures were hot, softened only by torrential rains and often dense cloud cover. Governed by Australia before the war, the population consisted almost exclusively of native islanders. A few coconut plantations and missionary settlements reflected inroads of western civilization, but for the most part the islands remained primitive.

The *Japanese Eighth Army* headquarters directed operations in the archipelago. From Rabaul, it controlled all *Japanese Army* forces in the Solomons, New Guinea, and the Bismarcks. By late 1943, following the series of defeats which had begun in Papua and Guadalcanal and continued through the battles for North-East New Guinea and the Solomons, the Japanese adopted a posture of strategic defense. Constant reinforcements brought the strength of the Rabaul garrison, the southeast anchor of their defensive perimeter, to over 90,000 men by February 1944, and additional units defended the outlying islands.

On the Allied side, General MacArthur's Southwest Pacific Area included Australia, the Netherlands East Indies from Java eastward, the Philippines, the Bismarck Archipelago, and New Guinea. As commander in chief of the region, MacArthur had operational control of army, navy, marine, and air force components from contributing Allied nations. For the Bismarck Archipelago Campaign, he drew most of his ground forces from Lt. Gen. Walter Krueger's U.S. Sixth Army. Lt. Gen. George Kenney commanded the Allied air forces, composed of the U.S. Fifth Air Force and elements from the Royal Australian Air Force. MacArthur's naval element, commanded by Vice Adm. Thomas Kinkaid, consisted primarily of vessels from the U.S. Seventh Fleet, augmented by ships from British Commonwealth nations.

MacArthur's area of responsibility was one of three major Allied theaters in the Pacific. To his north and east was a largely maritime theater, the Pacific Ocean Areas, under the command of Admiral Nimitz. To his east, Admiral William (Bull) Halsey commanded the South Pacific Area, a subtheater under Nimitz. Having successfully liberated the Solomon Islands from Guadalcanal to Bougainville, Halsey now threatened Rabaul from the east and south. During the Bismarck Archipelago Campaign, Halsey would respond to "strategic direction" from MacArthur but would continue to report to Nimitz.

Operations

To isolate Rabaul while gaining the logistical bases from which to support operations, MacArthur developed specific objectives for the Bismarck Archipelago Campaign. First, he wanted to gain control of the Vitiaz and Dampier Straits, which separate New Guinea and New Britain, by landing forces on the southwestern edge of New Britain. Second, he wanted Admiral Halsey to seize the Green Islands, located on the northwest edge of the Solomon Island chain approximately 117 miles east of Rabaul, as a base for air attacks against the Japanese fortress. Third, and perhaps most important from a tactical standpoint, was the seizure of the Admiralty Islands, located some 350 miles northwest of Rabaul, which would complete the encirclement of the Japanese base and provide the Allies with operational and logistic bases. An additional objective, capture of the Japanese base at Kavieng, New Ireland, was later changed to occupation of the undefended Emirau Island. (The latter site met Allied tactical and logistical requirements and did not entail the effort and human cost involved in an assault on a fortified base that could be neutralized by isolation.) To soften up the Japanese before the campaign began, the Allies initiated an air offensive against Rabaul from bases in the newly liberated Solomons and North-East New Guinea.

General MacArthur decided formally to open the campaign, Operation DEXTERITY, with December assaults on the western tip of New Britain. Possession of this area would provide the Allies with Cape Gloucester and the small harbor of Arawe, facilitating control of the Vitiaz and Dampier Straits. Local beaches were suitable for amphibious landings, and Japanese defenses were expected to be light.

General Krueger's Sixth Army was responsible for operations. Krueger selected the 112th Cavalry Regiment, plus artillery, engineers, and other supporting forces, to conduct the amphibious landing. First organized in 1920 as a horse cavalry unit, the 112th Cavalry had been converted to dismounted status in early 1943. Consequently, despite some hurried practice landings the unit was generally inexperienced in amphibious assault techniques. The landing plan called for the main assault to occur at the tip of the Arawe peninsula, while a company-size unit (A Troop) landed at the base of the peninsula in rubber boats to block a Japanese retreat.

The assault began on 15 December 1943 and almost immediately encountered severe difficulties. Japanese machine gunners spotted the rubber boats and sank almost all of them. The soldiers of A Troop were forced to abandon their equipment and swim for their lives. Sixteen were killed and seventeen wounded in this abortive attack before naval gunfire could silence the Japanese machine guns. Meanwhile, the main attack, employing conventional landing craft less susceptible to damage from machine gun fire, also ran into problems as successive landing waves became separated and confused. Nevertheless, superior Allied

Troops of the 32d Division near Saidor. (National Archives)

firepower forced the numerically inferior Japanese to retreat. By midafternoon the Americans controlled the peninsula.

Although they lost the opening battle, the Japanese did not concede Arawe to the Americans without further struggle. Beginning on the afternoon of the invasion, 15 December, and continuing for the next several days, they launched furious air attacks, especially targeting ships that had supported the assault. In addition, two nearby Japanese infantry battalions advanced on Arawe and dug in just beyond the American perimeter.

The tactical situation rapidly degenerated into a stalemate as the Americans and Japanese probed each other's lines. American strength and the natural defensive terrain along the base of the Arawe peninsula rendered the U.S. lodgment relatively secure for the moment, but American commanders could not feel comfortable with an entrenched enemy just outside their perimeter. To break the stalemate without incurring excessive casualties, Krueger landed a Marine Corps tank company and additional infantry to reinforce the 112th Cavalry. Employing the armor protection and firep wer provided by the tanks, the Americans drove the Japanese from their trenches on 16 January. Thereafter, Arawe was quiet. The victory had been achieved at a cost of 118 Americans killed, 352 wounded, and 4 missing.

While the operations on Arawe were under way, Krueger had developed plans to seize the Japanese airfield and garrison at Cape Gloucester on the western tip of New Britain. He assigned this mission to the 1st Marine Division, combat veterans of Guadalcanal. Because enemy defenses were concentrated near the airfiel , the marines landed on an undefended beach about six miles to the east on 26 December 1943. Once ashore, they advanced to the airfield along a narrow strip of dry ground. Japanese resistance was surprisingly light, and the marines controlled the airfield by 29 December. Japanese aircraft did manage to inflict some damage on the amphibious assault force supporting the operation, sinking one destroyer and damaging other support ships.

The heaviest combat came after the marines had secured the airfield. While clearing the Japanese from the jungles to the east, they encountered fierce opposition. The worst fighting came on New Year's Day, along a stream later dubbed Suicide Creek. The Japanese had constructed a well-camouflaged bunker complex along the stream bank and succeeded in repelling Marine attacks for two days. Finally, engineers constructed a corduroy road by laying logs over the mud so that tanks could be brought in to destroy the Japanese defenders. Although this initiative was successful, the price of victory was high. Marine casualties totaled 310 killed and 1,083 wounded.

By mid-January 1944 MacArthur's forces had secured the Vitiaz and Dampier Straits and were fi mly established on the western end of New Britain. At the same time, an Allied advance against Saidor,

1st Cavalry Division troops en route to the Admiralties. (National Archives)

North-East New Guinea, had given them a base beyond the other side of the straits and thus secured unhampered access to the Bismarck Sea. Yet western New Britain's utility as a forward operating and support base proved less critical to the Allied campaign than originally anticipated. The commander of the American PT boat squadron in the area declined to establish a base at Arawe, and Allied pilots preferred to use the airfields at Cape Gloucester. On 24 April the 40th Infantry

Division, a National Guard unit with soldiers from California, Utah, and Nevada, relieved the marines and 112th Cavalry. For the remainder of the campaign, the 40th Division would conduct patrols to keep the Japanese away from the western end of New Britain while the main Allied offensives continued elsewhere.

As the Allies advanced in the Central Pacific and Nimitz pressed his carrier attacks on Truk in the Carolines in mid-February 1944, the

Japanese began to reposition their air forces. The enemy aircraft remaining on New Guinea harassed the Americans but were too few to have much impact on Allied operations. The battles for Arawe and Cape Gloucester marked the last time that Japanese air power played a significant role in the Bismarck campaign

While MacArthur's forces regrouped and began preparations for the next phase of their drive toward Rabaul, Admiral Halsey's elements were on the move. Having initiated devastating attacks on Rabaul from carrier-based aircraft, Halsey sought a land base from which to continue these raids and to initiate PT boat attacks against Rabaul and New Ireland. One suitable location was the Green Islands. From them, PT boats could reach Rabaul and the southeastern coast of New Ireland, while land-based fighter planes could continue the air attacks on Rabaul and extend operations all the way up the New Ireland coast to Kavieng.

In February 1944 Halsey assigned the Green Islands operation to the 3d New Zealand Division, with support provided by the U.S. Navy. On 15 February the New Zealanders landed on Nissan, the largest of the islands, and over the next few days effectively eliminated all Japanese resistance. Shortly thereafter, construction battalions began building the airfields and PT boat bases Hals y had envisioned.

MacArthur's forces conducted the next operation in the Bismarck Archipelago Campaign. Its target was the Admiralty Islands. Success there would complete the encirclement of Rabaul and provide bases to support MacArthur's eventual thrust into the Philippines. In January 1944 a dramatic advance in breaking Japanese military codes within the ULTRA system played a prominent role in MacArthur's decisions regarding not only the Admiralties campaign but also his entire strategic concept.

The Admiralties are composed of two principal islands, Manus and Los Negros, and a number of smaller islands. Manus has steep mountains, dense jungle, and a few coconut plantations. Los Negros, smaller than Manus, is generally flat, with hills only in the southwest. Manus and Los Negros are separated by a narrow strait that forms a horseshoe-shaped curve. The interior of this curve, Seeadler Harbour, is one of the finest natural anchorages in the southern Pacific.

General Krueger assigned the Admiralties mission to the 1st Cavalry Division, commanded by Maj. Gen. Innis Swift. Organized under a prewar concept called the "square" division, it had two brigades, each consisting of two regiments with two squadrons in each regiment. The 1st Brigade was composed of the 5th and 12th Cavalry regiments, while the 2d Brigade consisted of the 7th and 8th Cavalry regiments.

Admiral Kinkaid and General MacArthur aboard the USS Phoenix. (National Archives)

The division had spent the first years of the war guarding the Mexican border and arrived in the Pacific in the latter half of 1943. Although the Admiralties operation would be its first combat action, its soldiers had received extensive training to prepare them for their mission.

Allied planners had originally scheduled the operation for 1 April to allow Admiral Nimitz to divert ships from the Central Pacific to support the campaign. As a result of ULTRA information, General Kenney's pilots on 24 January destroyed a squadron of Japanese planes that had deployed to Los Negros only two days earlier. Subsequent air operations in the area revealed that Japanese pilots had abandoned the area for safer bases. On 23 February, three B–25 medium bombers fl w over Manus and Los Negros for almost an hour at near treetop level without seeing any signs of enemy activity. Based on this report and other indications of a general Japanese withdrawal, notwithstanding ULTRA messages to the contrary, MacArthur decided to accelerate his operational schedule. He ordered a reconnaissance-in-force to probe Los Negros. If the island was undefended, additional forces were to land on the island; in the event of significant opposition, the reconnaissance unit would withdraw.

General Krueger received MacArthur's guidance on 24 February and with his subordinates initiated necessary planning. The 2d Squadron, 5th Cavalry, with supporting artillery, antiaircraft, and medical units, was selected to spearhead the operation. Brig. Gen. William Chase, commander of the 1st Brigade, assumed operational command of the task force, which was code-named BREWER. The Navy provided three destroyer-transports and nine destroyers to support the landing. The troops were packed into destroyers because they were the only ships available that could meet MacArthur's expedited timetable.

An indication that the operation might prove more difficult than anticipated came on 27 February when a six-man reconnaissance patrol landed on Los Negros. They reported that the island was "lousy" with Japanese. MacArthur's headquarters disregarded this report after General Kenney, the Fifth Air Force commander, argued that the information was too vague to justify changing the operational plan. In fact, according to ULTRA intercepts, the Japanese had 3,250 men in the Admiralties. (This figure was 400 short of the actual strength verified in postwar documents.) The patrol had encountered part of this substantial garrison defending the islands. Two infantry battalions, a transportation regiment, and some naval forces were so well camouflaged that the low-flying Allied reconnaissance planes had not detected their presence. It was only after Task Force BREWER landed that MacArthur's headquarters would become aware of the extent of the enemy presence on Los Negros.

The operation's momentum prevailed as the 1st Cavalry Division continued its preparations for the landings. MacArthur decided to witness the initial assault so that he could personally determine whether the operation should continue or be aborted. Subsequently, Admiral Kinkaid designated the light cruiser, *Phoenix*, to serve as the general's command ship. Its crew was scattered throughout Brisbane, Australia, on shore leave when the order to sail arrived. Navy trucks with loudspeakers had to drive through the city streets to announce the urgent recall. The sailors rushed to their ship, which final y sailed with most of its crew on board. Kinkaid joined MacArthur on the *Phoenix* to view the amphibious assault.

On the morning of 29 February 1944, U.S. forces assaulted Hyane Harbour, located on the east side of Los Negros. The site was close to Momote Plantation airfield, one of the early assault objectives. The Japanese had not anticipated a landing there because the harbor had a narrow entrance and a small beach. The bulk of their forces were concentrated on the other side of the island to defend the beaches of

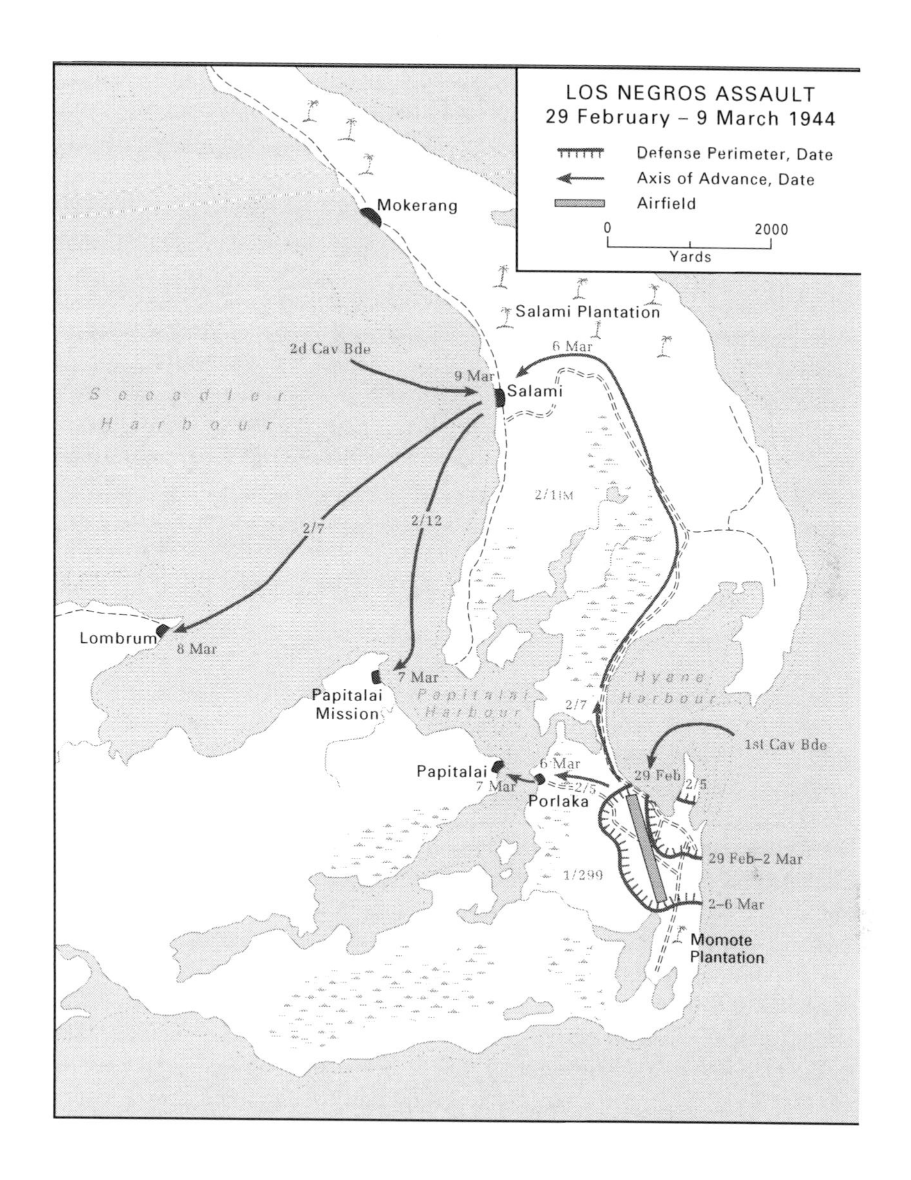

Seeadler Harbour. Only a few coast artillery and antiaircraft batteries and machine guns were positioned to oppose the initial assault.

At 0817, the first wave of boats landed at Hyane Harbour. Japanese gunners on both sides of the mouth of the harbor continued to fire on the next three waves of landing craft, but naval gunfire and a driving rain limited their effectiveness. The landings proceeded on schedule with only four boats sustaining damage. By shortly after noon the entire reconnaissance force was ashore and had secured a small perimeter around Momote Plantation airfield. Reconnaissance patrols did not encounter any Japanese troops but found ample evidence of enemy activity.

General MacArthur came ashore some time after 1500. He inspected the perimeter area, awarded a Distinguished Service Cross to 2d Lt. Marvin Henshaw, who was the first American on the beach, and expressed his satisfaction with the operation's progress. Before leaving he told General Chase: "You have all performed marvelously. Hold what you have taken, no matter against what odds. You have your teeth in him now—don't let go."

After MacArthur and the bulk of the Navy task force departed—two destroyers remained on station to provide fire support—the cavalrymen began to prepare for Japanese attacks. Lacking barbed wire, Chase contracted his perimeter to secure only half of the airfield and ordered his men to dig in. The soldiers soon discovered that preparing positions in the coral of Los Negros was a tedious task, requiring picks and shovels to make any progress. All, however, remained optimistic that the Japanese reaction would be relatively minor.

Meanwhile, the Japanese on the island were also making preparations. Col. Yoshio Ezaki, their commander, issued the following order to the battalion nearest Hyane Harbour: "Tonight the battalion under Captain Baba will annihilate the enemy who have landed. This is not a delaying action. Be resolute to sacrifice your life for the Emperor and commit suicide in case capture is imminent. We must carry out our mission and annihilate the enemy on the spot. I am highly indignant about the enemy's arrogant attitude. Remember to kill or capture all ranking officers for intelligence pu poses."

Fortunately for the Americans, Ezaki continued to believe that the main Allied attack would come on the other side of the island at Seeadler Harbour and so he committed only limited forces against the dug-in cavalrymen. The attacks began after dark, when the Japanese attempted to infiltrate through the American lines in small groups. The cavalrymen remained in their foxholes, shooting at anything that moved. Although the integrity of the defensive position was maintained, some Japanese crawled between foxholes to penetrate the perimeter. Two enemy soldiers managed to reach the task force command post, but Maj. Julio Chiarmonte, the task force S–2, heard their voices and killed one and wounded the other with his submachine gun.

Pfc. Walter Hawks of E Troop exemplified the bravery of the cavalrymen who fought that night. Occupying a foxhole forward of the perimeter, he observed a group of Japanese soldiers setting up a machine gun to support the attack. Knowing that he would reveal his position, he nevertheless fired and killed the entire group. He then had to fend off Japanese attacks the rest of the night. Hawks' situation was not unique. When a group of Japanese soldiers infiltrated the perimeter from the ocean by swimming around the end of the American lines and attacking from the rear, elements of the 3d Platoon of E Troop found themselves similarly isolated and fightin for survival the rest of the night.

The hours of darkness were particularly long for the wounded. The task force had established a portable surgical facility ashore in an abandoned enemy position, and lanterns and flashlights were assembled so that medical personnel could work throughout the night. Instruments were sterilized in a bucket over a fire. Because of the intense fighting and the fluidity of the situation, some of the wounded were forced to remain in their foxholes overnight. By morning, 7 Americans had been killed and 15 were wounded; the Americans counted 66 Japanese dead within their perimeter.

With the coming of dawn on 1 March, Japanese attacks ceased, allowing the Americans to capture infiltrators who remained inside the perimeter, including a few who had reoccupied fortified bunkers. Chase also dispatched patrols outside the perimeter to locate the enemy and used their findings and intelligence from captured documents to provide targets for naval gunfire and American bombers.

By midafternoon the Japanese had renewed their pressure on the Americans. A fifteen-man unit commanded by Captain Baba, which may have infiltrated the previous evening, appeared inside the perimeter. Charging the task force command post, the unit was cut down by heavy American fire. Rather than surrender, the Japanese survivors committed suicide. The Americans easily repulsed a late-afternoon attack on the perimeter as well as small-unit probes that night. On 2 March, the second morning ashore, the cavalrymen breathed easier.

The rest of the 5th Regiment landed on Los Negros on 2 March, along with the 99th Artillery Battalion, the 40th Naval Construction Battalion (Seabees), and other support troops. Landing ship, tanks (LSTs) unloaded heavy equipment, ammunition, kitchens, and other needed supplies directly on the beach. General Chase expanded the perimeter to encompass the entire airfield in order to accommodate these reinforcements. The Seabees, who fought as infantrymen when necessary, formed an inner perimeter. Artillery and mortar positions were prepared and fire planning further coordinated with the destroyers offshore.

Supplies and equipment are loaded aboard amphibious craft at Seeadler Harbour. (National Archives)

The arrival of the reinforcements convinced Colonel Ezaki that the American main effort was in fact at Hyane Harbour. He planned an attack on the Los Negros perimeter for the night of 2 March but delayed it for twenty-four hours when American artillery and naval gunfire prevented him from massing his forces. The fighting which final y occurred on the night of 3 March proved to be the most critical during the battle for the Admiralties.

The 3 March Japanese attack on the American perimeter started about 2100. Although the entire American line was engaged, the weary soldiers of the 2d Squadron, 5th Cavalry, once more bore the brunt of the enemy assaults. Withering fire from the cavalrymen killed scores of Japanese, but the enemy pressed his attacks throughout the night. Fire support from artillery, mortars, and naval guns played a crucial role in breaking up the Japanese onslaughts. The captain of the destroyer USS *Mullany* brought his ship close enough to the shore to, in his words, "hit 'em with a potato" as his gunners directed intense barrages at advancing Japanese formations.

Throughout the evening the cavalrymen reported hearing the Japanese relaying false commands in English. An unsuspecting mortar section abandoned its position when it heard an American voice directing a retreat. Other soldiers reported that the Japanese were tapping into telephone lines and giving false orders and reports. One mortar battery refused an urgent plea in clear English to cease firing when the caller was unable to identify himself. Most other spurious communications were also ignored.

Heroism, such as that displayed by Sgt. Troy McGill of G Troop, was not uncommon. His squad was defending a revetment about thirty-five yards in front of the main perimeter when the Japanese launched an attack. Soon, all but McGill and one other soldier were killed. The sergeant ordered his companion to escape to the perimeter while he continued to defend the position. When his rifle jammed, he used it as a club until he was killed. Subsequently, McGill was awarded the Medal of Honor for his courage and selflessness

Near dawn, the Seabees left their foxholes to reinforce the battered cavalrymen along the perimeter. As they advanced, they encountered a Japanese soldier inside the perimeter who had taken over a U.S. machine gun position. A few Seabees quickly dispatched the enemy and recovered the position, while their compatriots manned another gun position near the beach. The night engagements were a harrowing experience for everyone inside the perimeter.

By daybreak on 4 March the worst of the fighting was over. Although sporadic mortar and artillery fire continued for some time, the Americans had withstood the best the Japanese could throw at them. Over 750 enemy soldiers lay dead on the field of battle, as compared to 61 Americans. There were no prisoners. The Japanese had obeyed orders to commit suicide rather than surrender.

In defeating a numerically superior enemy, the men of the 5th Cavalry had secured a solid foothold on Los Negros. They inflicte such heavy casualties that the Japanese were unable to launch another

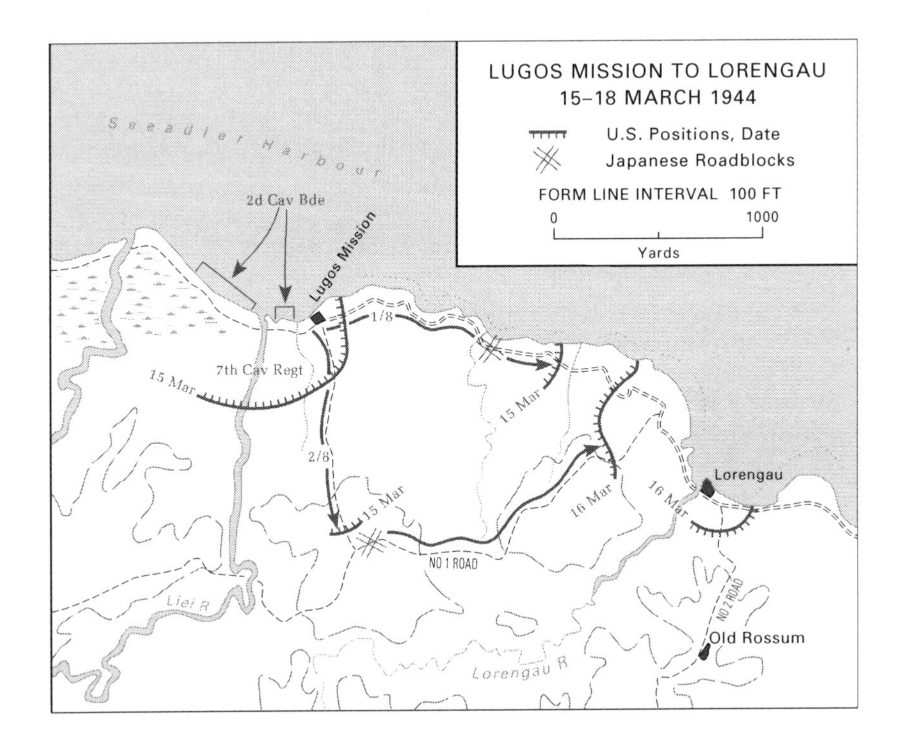

attack of similar magnitude on the Los Negros perimeter. To be sure, another month of hard fighting lay ahead of the division, but there was no longer any question about the outcome. For its actions on Los Negros, the 2d Squadron, 5th Cavalry Regiment, received the Distinguished Unit Citation.

The arrival of the 2d Squadron, 7th Cavalry, on 4 March was a welcome relief. The following day, General Swift, the division commander, assumed direct command of the growing force. On 6 March the landing of the 12th Regiment with supporting artillery, tanks, and engineers gave the Americans the necessary combat power to launch offensive operations. Swift directed his attention to clearing the Japanese from the eastern beaches of Los Negros so that Seeadler Harbour could be opened to accommodate the landing of the division's other brigade. The 2d Squadron, 7th Cavalry, moved northward on 5 March and was joined by the 12th Cavalry the following day. Throughout the four-mile advance, Japanese resistance was light, and fallen trees and mud proved to be the most difficult obstacles. The large quantities of captured enemy supplies reflected the disintegration of the Japanese defense force following the disastrous defeat on the night of 3 March.

With the interior beaches secured, Swift moved to seize three promontories on the interior of Seeadler Harbour from which the Japanese could interfere with the impending landings. He ordered the 5th Cavalry to move west to take Papitalai; the 2d Squadron, 12th Cavalry, to seize Papitalai Mission by moving across the bay in small amphibious craft; and the 2d Squadron, 7th Cavalry, to seize Lombrum Plantation, also by moving across the bay in amphibious craft. The opposition at Papitalai was ineffective, and the Japanese abandoned Lombrum Plantation before the Americans arrived. But the effort to take Papitalai Mission proved more difficult.

The 2d Squadron, 12th Cavalry, did not begin its movement until the afternoon of 7 March, and by evening only G Troop had landed near the objective. With further reinforcement impossible in the dark, the company-size force had to defend itself against three night counterattacks, surviving only with the help of well-placed artillery support. The next morning the rest of the squadron landed at the mission and cleared the area of Japanese.

American control of the beaches and principal promontories on Los Negros did not ensure unimpeded access to Seeadler Harbour. Well-hidden Japanese batteries on the small islands at the mouth of the harbor were able to engage ships entering and leaving the anchorage despite the continued efforts of the Allies. For some weeks, Allied warships had bombarded these positions and silenced their fire only to encounter renewed shelling the next time they returned. Once navy commanders discovered that the Japanese were reluctant to engage Allied vessels beyond 10,000 yards because of a shortage of ammunition, they undertook a deliberate bombardment from a greater range and succeeded in eliminating all Japanese resistance within a few days.

With the approaches to Seeadler Harbour secured, the 2d Brigade landed on Los Negros, followed by medical units, engineers, supply units, and other support forces. Concurrently, the Seabees made Momote Plantation airfield operational, allowing Royal Australian Air Force units to conduct air operations from the facility as early as 10 March. Following elimination of the few remaining Japanese on Los Negros, General Swift turned his attention toward the larger island of Manus.

Swift gave Brig. Gen. Verne Mudge, commander of the 2d Brigade, 1st Cavalry Division, the task of capturing Manus. Mudge's cavalrymen faced a formidable task. The steep terrain and dense jungle were believed to conceal well-fortified pillboxes that would have to be eliminated through painfully slow and potentially costly assaults.

But before attacking Manus directly, the American commander wanted to secure the small islands of Butjo Mokau and Hauwei for use as artillery bases. From there, artillery could fire perpendicular to the projected landing area and the axis of advance, a technique that would allow reasonable support with less-than-precise gun accuracy.

Butjo Mokau was undefended and easily occupied, but Hauwei proved more difficult. On 11 March a landing craft supported by a PT boat landed a platoon-size reconnaissance force on the latter island. Shortly after entering the jungle, the unit was ambushed. After fightin their way for over two hours back to the beach, the Americans discovered that the PT boat, whose skipper had been wounded in the landing, had withdrawn. The landing craft, which had remained nearby, attempted to extract the cavalrymen, but it hit a submerged reef as it pulled away from the beach and sank. Eighteen wounded survivors floated in the water for more than three hours until they were picked up by a PT boat.

Despite this initial setback, General Swift was determined to take the island. On 12 March the 2d Squadron, 7th Cavalry, preceded by a naval barrage and Australian Air Force strikes, assaulted Hauwei in force. The Japanese resisted from well-prepared and concealed jungle fortifications, but the arrival of a single tank on 13 March turned the tide for the cavalrymen. Without antitank weapons, the Japanese could not stop the lone armored vehicle and Hauwei was soon taken. Eight Americans were killed and forty-six wounded in the operation, while forty-three Japanese sailors lost their lives. The value of Hauwei as an artillery base during subsequent operations, however, justified the cost of capturing the island.

With the artillery in position, the cavalrymen were ready to attack Manus. General Swift designated Lorengau airfield on Manus as a primary objective, but it was too strongly defended to be taken by a frontal assault. Therefore, he decided to land at Lugos Mission, about two and one-half miles west of the airfiel , with the 8th Cavalry leading and the 7th Cavalry in reserve. The 15 March assault went well. Encountering only light resistance, the 8th Regiment quickly turned toward Lorengau along two axes. Its 1st Squadron proceeded east along a coastal route called Number 3 Road to approach Lorengau from the seaward side, while the 2d Squadron moved inland and turned east along a dirt trail called Number 1 Road to reach the airfiel from the island interior.

Progress for the squadrons was unequal. Inland, the 2d Squadron moved steadily through the jungle, reducing Japanese bunkers en route with the aid of tanks. The 1st Squadron, however, encountered formidable resistance from prepared bunkers. Shortly before noon the squadron's progress was halted by extremely heavy fire from a line of well-fortified pillboxes. Concentrated artillery fire from Hauwei failed to reduce the bunkers, but Australian planes based on Los Negros demolished the positions with 500-pound bombs. The 1st Squadron then advanced to the edge of Lorengau airfield where it halted for the night.

The next morning, 16 March, the 1st Squadron launched an assault on the airfield but was quickly halted by a series of pillboxes located along the southern edge of the runway. C Troop attacked the position, while the rest of the squadron attempted to maneuver around the Japanese. One platoon of C Troop, through a flanking attack, reached the bunkers and began tossing grenades into the position. However, when Japanese soldiers began firing at B Troop, maneuvering nearby, confusion ensued. As the B Troop soldiers returned the Japanese fire, some of their rounds hit C Troop soldiers. Under fire from its own comrades, C Troop withdrew, and the squadron commander wisely stopped the advance for the day, with half of the airfiel still in enemy hands.

That evening, General Mudge replaced the tired 1st Squadron soldiers with fresh cavalrymen from the 7th Regiment. He also ordered a heavy naval and mortar bombardment, supported by the artillery on Hauwei. When the 7th Regiment soldiers attacked the next morning, they discovered that the bombardment had been extremely effective. In the face of very weak Japanese resistance, the Americans swept across the airfield to the nearby Lorengau River, where they linked up with the 2d Squadron of the 8th Regiment emerging from the jungle. The airfield as secure.

On the far side of the Lorengau River lay the village of Lorengau, another military objective. American concern that the Japanese might make a determined stand there evaporated on 18 March when enemy resistance crumbled under artillery and mortar fire. The cavalrymen easily occupied the village, but the battle for Manus was not over.

Pushed from the airfield and the village of Lorengau, the Japanese retreated into the island's interior. There, at a village called Old Rossum, they constructed a complex of pillbox fortifications and prepared to make a final stand. Mudge directed the 7th Regiment, supported by the 8th Regiment, to clear the approaches to the village. But from 19–25 March, some 200 Japanese effectively frustrated the effort, fighting from position to position along the narrow Rossum Road corridor and giving ground only when necessary. Finally, American determination and the support of air and artillery overcame enemy resistance; the road was opened and the village occupied. Thereafter, organized Japanese resistance crumbled. Some survivors retreated into the jungles. Hunted by natives and American soldiers, the Japanese wandered aimlessly, subsisting on dog meat and native gardens. A few surrendered, but most were either killed or died in the jungles.

Following the end of Japanese resistance on Manus, only mopping-up actions and the capture of tiny garrisons on the smaller islands remained to be accomplished until the Admiralties were considered secure. The mop-up operations had little military significance, with one notable exception. On 1 April, cavalrymen in native dug-out canoes assaulted the small islands of Koruniat and Ndrilo, marking the only time in the Pacific campaign such vessels were used to conduct an amphibious assault.

But the Allies had problems other than the enemy, terrain, and weather. When the shooting at Manus stopped, infighting began among the ranking Americans over the issue of base command and control. Admiral Nimitz wanted Halsey to supervise base construction, reporting directly to him, because the Navy was furnishing most of the construction personnel. Since the base was within MacArthur's area of responsibility, the Joint Chiefs of Staff quickly disapproved this proposal. However, angered by the Navy's position, MacArthur unilaterally decided to limit use of the Admiralty bases to naval forces under his command (i.e., the Seventh Fleet and Royal Australian Navy). To resolve the dispute, Halsey and some of his staff fl w to MacArthur's headquarters. After two days of heated but unproductive discussions, the exasperated admiral told MacArthur that the general had placed his personal honor before the welfare of the United States. Stunned, MacArthur responded: "My God, Bull. You can't really mean that? We can't have anything like that." MacArthur reversed his decision and allowed all Allied ships to use Seeadler Harbour.

With the command issue settled, the leaders turned their attention back to the war. Air, naval, and army bases were completed, and the Admiralties became a major support center. As one of the largest naval bases in the Pacific, Seeadler Harbour serviced the Third, Fifth, and Seventh Fleets and Royal Australian Navy vessels. Its repair facilities, petroleum depots, and other naval support activities were vital to the continued offensive. Meanwhile, from the airfields of Los Negros, the Allies struck Japanese targets on New Guinea and the Carolines. At the same time, the Army moved hospitals, field depots, and other support units into the Admiralties and prepared to use the islands as a staging area for the eventual invasion of the Philippines.

With the Admiralties captured, the Allies entered the final phase of the Bismarck Archipelago Campaign. MacArthur wanted Halsey to attack the Japanese base at Kavieng. The admiral, however, argued that the Japanese withdrawal from the region diminished the importance of Kavieng and that a costly assault was unnecessary. In his view, the Allies could isolate Kavieng and establish a forward support base on a smaller island. With the support of Admiral Nimitz, Halsey convinced the Joint Chiefs of Staff to change the final campaign objective from Kavieng to Emirau, an island located midway between Kavieng and the Admiralties that was thought to be lightly defended. On 14 March the newly created 4th Marine Regiment assaulted Emirau and found the island unoccupied. The Americans immediately started building air and PT boat facilities there. From Emirau, American bombers could reach the Carolines, and PT boats could patrol the northern coast of New Ireland.

With the occupation of Emirau, all the objectives of the Bismarck Archipelago Campaign had been realized. Within four months, the Allies had converted the archipelago from a barrier to a stepping-stone in the advance toward the Philippines. Rabaul and Kavieng remained under Japanese control, but they were surrounded and impotent. The Admiralties, with Seeadler Harbour, provided the Allies with a superb logistical base and an extremely important naval facility from which to pursue operations against the enemy.

Analysis

The Bismarck Archipelago Campaign would formally end for the United States Army on 27 November 1944, although Australian soldiers would continue combat operations on New Britain long after the Americans had moved on toward the Philippines. By the end of the Army campaign, fully developed logistical and support bases were completed and operating in support of subsequent operations. In marked contrast to the frustrations of earlier campaigns, such as Papua and Guadalcanal, in the Bismarck Archipelago the Allies had achieved all of their objectives on time or even ahead of schedule, with a minimum of casualties.

The unique geography of this area of operations and the detailed intelligence data provided by ULTRA, as well as MacArthur's leadership style, contributed to rapid and relatively inexpensive victories. Although initially opposed to bypassing Japanese strongpoints like Rabaul, MacArthur and his staff soon came to realize the value of such tactics. The general used his air and naval forces to maneuver around Japanese strongpoints, avoiding the delays and heavy casualties that would have resulted from frontal assaults on well-fortified enemy positions. This policy frustrated the Japanese, who were unable to defend every island in strength, and allowed the Allies to concentrate on the weakest points in the Japanese defense. The nearly impregnable fortress at Rabaul did little for the Japanese because MacArthur isolated it and passed it by.

Formidable fighters as individuals, the Japanese did not have the resources to oppose the Allied drive. Their soldiers fought with intense determination, but dedication alone was not enough. As the war progressed, an increasing lack of ships and aircraft prevented them from maneuvering against the Allies and attacking vulnerable amphibious assault operations. When MacArthur launched the invasion of the Admiralties, the Japanese could neither reinforce nor protect the islands. Defeat was almost inevitable.

In the final analysis, the American home front, the source of a seemingly unending fl w of supplies and equipment, combined with the fighting skills of the American soldier to make victory possible. The men of the Sixth Army and the Marine Corps fought with determination and daring, often against superior numbers. Supported by Seabees on the ground and skilled U.S. and Australian aviators and sailors, the Allied soldiers prevailed where lesser men might have failed. Victory went to the strong and able. The road to the Philippines was opening.

Made in the USA
Middletown, DE
05 March 2023